Spirit Dance

a colouring book

by

Ambika Gail Rutherford

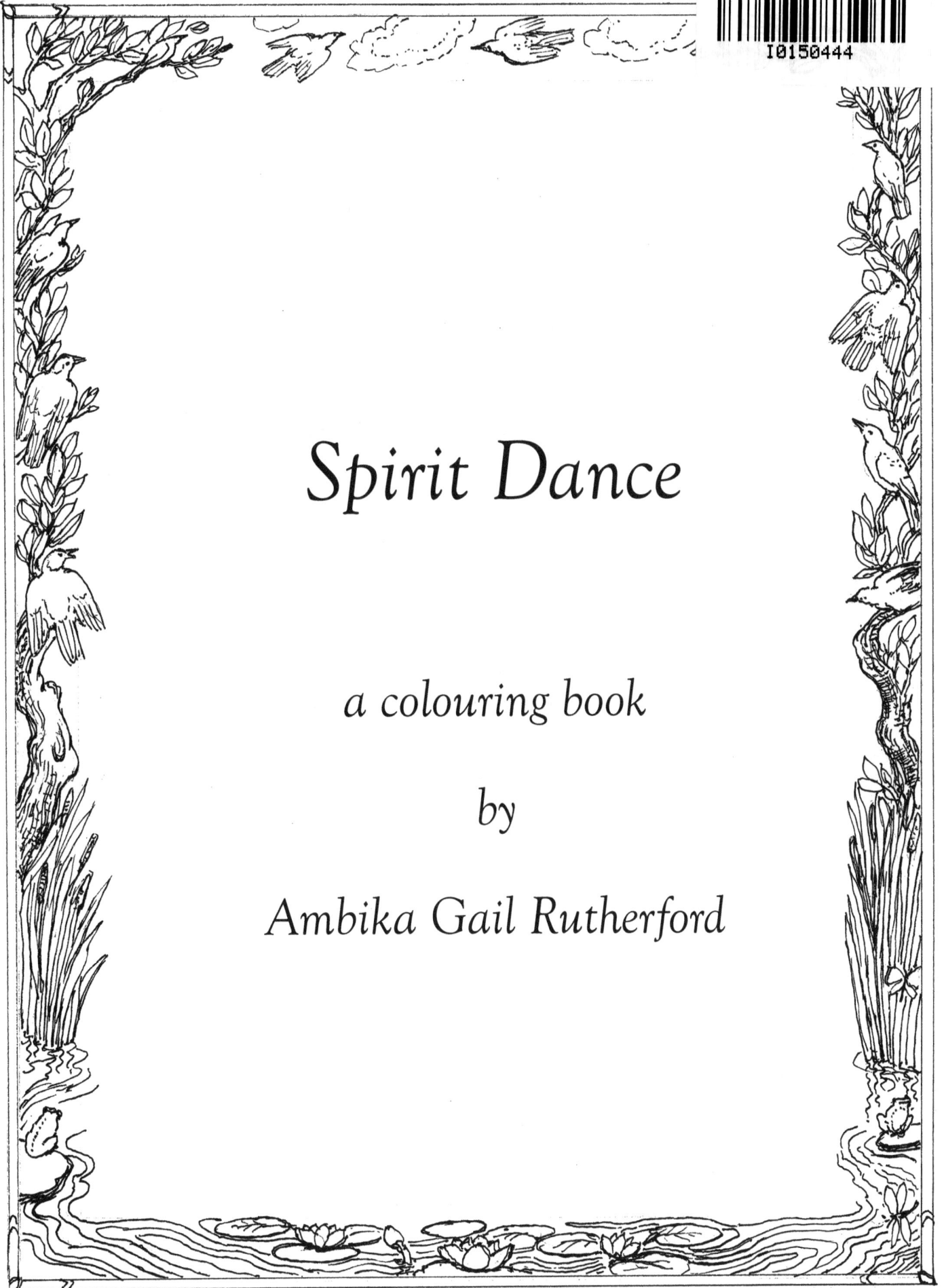

First published in 2016 by Underhill Books in Charlottetown, Prince Edward Island

ISBN: 978-09950270-22

Underhill Books
4183 Murray Harbour Drive
RR#3 Belfast PEI
C0A 1A0 Canada
www.underhillbooks.com

Author's Note

These drawings explore our relationship to the natural world, fantasy showing our interaction and interdependence with the earth and its creatures.

***

These illustrations are printed on one side of each page for convenience of colouring, on paper excellent for pencil crayons and also heavy enough to allow use of markers. If you wish to use many overlays of markers it will saturate the paper, so I recommend backing your colouring with a loose piece of copy paper to protect the next page.

the stars and all the galaxies run through her hands like beads.

There is a secret one inside ~ all the

stars and all the galaxies run through her hands like beads.

www.ingramcontent.com/pod-product-compliance
Lightning Source LLC
LaVergne TN
LVHW061302060426
835509LV00016B/1676